THE LINCOLN TRAIN IS COMING...

by

Wayne and Mary Cay Wesolowski

First Edition, 3rd Printing
Copyright ©1995, 2014
all rights reserved
Printed in China

ACKNOWLEDGEMENTS

Dr. Richard Becker, President, Illinois Benedictine College
Dr. William Carroll, President, Benedictine University
Robert R. McCormick (Chicago Tribune) Foundation
Union Pacific Foundations

James S. Copley Foundation, LaJolla, CA
Kalmbach Publishing, Inc., Waukesha, WI
Lincoln National Corporation, Ft. Wayne, IN
Santa Fe Southern Foundation, Schaumburg, IL
State Farm Mutual Insurance Companies, Bloomington, IL
D. Ray Wilson, Carpentersville, IL

Dr. Philip Bean
Sylvia Leeseberg
Mary Joyce Pickett
Colleen Sehy
Dr. Thomas Schwartz
John Kunzie
George Lamason Jr.
H. Robert Slusser
Don Snoddy
John Haines
James O'Toole
Orville Mohr
Dan Weinberg
Bruce & Pauline Bailey
Ed Bunting
Margaret Lant
Virgil Davis

    Our deepest thanks to all these and the many, many individuals and companies who made the Lincoln Train possible.

In memory of
Thomas Dyba
the Lincoln Home miniaturist
who first planted the seeds for
the Lincoln Train project

The original locomotive "Nashville" of the Cleveland Columbus and Cincinnati R.R. stands ready bedecked in bunting, special black-fringed presidential flags and a portrait of the fallen president for its trip from Cleveland to Columbus, OH (Library of Congress)

The model locomotive "Nashville" carries the same bunting and flags as the original. It was made from a three inch diameter plastic water pipe with many special urethane plastic castings. (W. Wesolowski)

4

The Lincoln Train
is Coming... The 1865 Funeral Trip

The assassin's bullet that ended the life of the 16th President of the United States also began one of the epic railroad journeys in history—the Abraham Lincoln Funeral Train. The North had barely begun the jubilant celebration of Lee's surrender and the end of the vicious Civil War when its soul was wrenched again with the killing of President Lincoln. The mourning of the entire nation was centered on a 1666-mile journey of a slow-moving funeral train. Leaving Washington on April 21, 1865 it would not reach Springfield, Illinois for fourteen days, moving through most of the major northern cities. At Washington, Baltimore, Harrisburg, Philadelphia, New York City, Albany, Buffalo, Cleveland, Columbus, Indianapolis, Chicago and Springfield the train stopped, the coffin was removed and huge formal processions would bring Lincoln's body to state capitals and city halls. There, for hours, thousands of sullen, often weeping, citizens would file by for one last glimpse of the open coffin and the fallen hero they most likely had never seen in life. The crowds, often twelve abreast, would move all night long with great dignity past the bier.

Since there was no mass media to deliver instant coverage the only way for the average citizen to participate was to come trackside and they did, by the millions. Charles King, a cadet at West Point Military Academy, wrote of his experience as the train came up the Hudson River valley, "A few days later we formed lines parallel with the railway over at Garrisons and with our drums and colors draped in black, stood at the present, as the day was dying and a long funeral train rolled slowly by. On the platforms, and at the car windows, were generals famous in song and story, but we all had eyes for only that solemn pile on which was laid all that was mortal of him who had become immortal, whose works and whose wisdom gain in worth and power with every added year, the inspiration of a reunited people so long as the flag shall float and the nation live."

Early in the morning of April 22, 1865 the train prepares to leave the Northern Central RR depot at Harrisburg, PA. (Pennsylvania State Archives)

Cleveland, Columbus & Cincinnati R. R.

SPECIAL TIME SCHEDULE

FOR THE TRAIN CONVEYING THE

REMAINS OF ABRAHAM LINCOLN, LATE PRESIDENT OF THE U.S., AND ESCORT,

FROM WASHINGTON, D. C., TO SPRINGFIELD, ILL.

Cleveland to Columbus, Saturday, April 29th, 1865.

Leave Cleveland	12.00	Midnight.
Berea	12.43	A. M.
Olmsted	12.51	"
Columbia	1.02	"
Grafton	1.23	"
La Grange	1.37	"
Wellington	2.00	"
Rochester	2.17	"
New London	2.36	"
Greenwich	2.59	"
Shiloh	3.19	"
Shelby	3.39	"
Crestline	4.07	"
Galion	4.23	"
Iberia	4.41	"
Gilead	5.05	"
Cardington	5.20	"
Ashley	5.43	"
Eden	5.55	"
Berlin	6.19	"
Lewis Centre	6.32	"
Orange	6.37	"
Worthington	6.56	"
Arrive Columbus	7.30	A. M.

This Train will have exclusive right to the Road against all other Trains. A Pilot Locomotive will be run ten minutes in advance of the above Schedule time.

E. S. FLINT, Superintendent.

Without radio or television to alert the people special timetables were printed for each section of the route. (Wesolowski Collection)

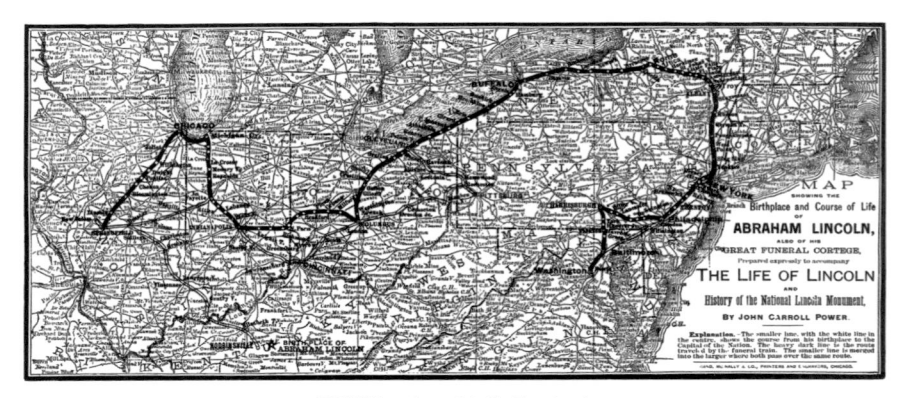

(BU/Wesolowski Collection)

Secretary of War Edwin Stanton with a "group of citizens" planned the route which basically retraced Lincoln's inaugural trip, skipping Pittsburgh. Cincinnati was also excluded because of the southern sympathizers and democrats there. A smaller freight route was used from Columbus to Indianapolis. The journey with both political and social implications was executed with precision by the military who could still demand control of the railroads. Special timetables were issued to inform the citizens of the route. Farmers and ordinary citizens left their fields and jobs to travel long distances just for a brief glimpse of the train.

(BU/Wesolowski Collection)

Huge floral arches praising Lincoln in life and in death were constructed over the tracks in many towns. The arch at Michigan City, IN read "With Tears We Resign Thee to God and History, The Purposes of the Almighty are Perfect, and Must Prevail." A forty-foot high arch in Chicago, constructed in just a few days, cost over $15,000. Funeral cities absorbed the cost of the services and tried to outdo each other in the size and quality of their funeral tribute. Young women dressed in white were frequently present and allowed, in a few rare cases, to enter the car and place flowers on the coffin. Bands played funeral dirges and thousands of bonfires lit the night with a yellow orange glow as even bareheaded strong men openly wept asking, "Would the violence ever end?" Riley Scott writing to his mother in May 1865 said, "I was at the depot when the funeral train came in. It was a solemn sight to see the train which bore the precious remains of one of the best men that ever lived on earth. I cannot describe the procession to you, it would take too long."

Orders to each railroad required guards at all high locations and strategic points with turnouts spiked in place. The train would have rights over all the traffic that would halt one hour before the special's arrival. A lead engine going ten minutes ahead of the train would alert the people of the approach of the Lincoln Train which was limited to 25 miles per hour and only 5 miles per hour in depots and places where people had gathered. Despite the length of the journey through seven states using 15 different railroads and two car ferries the train arrived in Springfield only one hour late.

Mrs. Lincoln was too distraught to even attend the funeral and asked that no photographs be taken of Lincoln in the coffin, although one print does exist. Robert Todd Lincoln, in a letter to the Union Pacific in 1905, said he did not ride his father's train, but traveled directly to Springfield by another route. Abraham did not, however, make the trip alone. His younger son, Willie, had died in Washington three years earlier of a fever. His small coffin was exhumed and made the trip together with his father in the same railroad car.

Funeral historians agree that the embalming practice of the time was adequate for the many open-coffin funerals despite bizarre claims to the contrary. It does appear that Stanton refused to allow morticians to apply makeup to the President's face to clearly show the damage of the head wound.

The great journey over, Abraham would be laid to rest on May 4, 1865 in a "quiet place" as he had requested. His life had ended, but his legacy and legend had only begun.

Sent from St. Louis, this grand hearse was used for the Springfield portion of the Lincoln funeral. (Illinois State Historical Library)

Constructed by the United States Military Railroad System at Alexandria, Virginia the President's private car. "United States" was perhaps one of the most opulent rail cars of its time. (Library of Congress)

From the beginning the train would be something never before equaled. No ordinary car would be used, but a special presidential car just completed, but never used by the President. Mr. Lincoln actually made fewer than six official trips by rail during his presidency, choosing instead to travel by boat to most military meetings. A noted exception was a spectacular trip to West Point, NY to consult with ailing General Winfield Scott. The New York Herald reported, "Thus, in only eleven hours the Chief Magistrate had traveled from Washington to West Point—a distance of nearly three hundred miles" at the fearsome speed of 27 mph.

Sometime in 1864 the construction of a special presidential car was authorized, probably by Brevet Brig. General Daniel McCallum, Director of the Military RR System. It was constructed at Alexandria, Virginia in the Car Shops of the Military RR System. Benjamin Patten Lamason was the Superintendent of Car Repair and designer of the car. William Henry Harrison Price was the shop foreman with direct responsibility for its construction. Perhaps following the custom of design for European royalty, it was one of the most opulent of its time. With sixteen wheels for a smoother ride, rounded monitor ends, fine woodwork, upholstered walls, etched glass windows, the "United States" represented the finest in car construction. Mr. Price clearly writes in Locomotive Engineering, September 1893 that no armor plating was used in the walls as later rumored. The car contained three rooms for work and sitting, but without cooking and long term sleeping facilities it was not designed for long range travel. The large scoop-like devices on the roof are for air movement over simple stoves at the ends of the car. Designed as a "compromise" car it had extra wide wheel tread for use on standard gauge up to, and including, five foot gauge that was common in both the north and south. A large United States crest was painted for the sides of the car since no official presidential seal existed at the time. Mr. Lincoln may have chosen not to use the car because it was too ornate for his style. General Herman Haupt of the USMRR stated, "The President himself never affected style or required anything more than ordinary accommodations."

One day before the trip Myron Lamson, among others, prepared the car with stars, tassels and bunting. To facilitate removal of the coffin at the various stops, one end railing was removed and replaced with a simple roller system. By McCallum's direct order B.P. Lamason accompanied the car on its first and only official trip.

Within one year the huge military railroad system was disbanded and returned to civilian control. The "United States" was sold despite some objection by Stanton for $6850 as an executive car to the Union Pacific Railroad. After less than eight years of service it was unceremoniously sold to the Colorado Central RR for $3000. Stripped of interior compartments it worked as a simple day coach with long wooden benches running along the still upholstered walls. Downgraded to a lowly work car and nearly derelict, the car was returned to the Union Pacific in the early 1890's. With some refurbishing it was displayed at the 1898 Trans-Mississippi Centennial transportation exhibit in Omaha. Kept in a protected barn at the UP shops, there is some record of an effort by the black citizens of Omaha to purchase and repair the car as a celebration of Lincoln's Emancipation Proclamation, but the project never came to fruition. Finally the UP sold the car to entrepreneur Franklyn Snow of Peoria, IL for $2000. Snow, who said his "business is a writer of advertisements and promoter of advertising ideas," successfully exhibited the car in the Lincoln Museum at the 1904 St. Louis World's Fair. His efforts to use the car as a commercial exhibit in the midwest were not successful and the car was sold for mechanics liens to former SOO Line president and interurban magnate Thomas Lowry.

Moved to a newly developed area outside Minneapolis, MN called Columbia Heights, Lowry promoted his exhibit as the "most sacred relic in the United States." The car underwent significant restoration and was housed in a fenced area. Unfortunately two boys were burning weeds as instructed on March 18, 1911 when a huge windstorm came up and the resulting prairie fire destroyed more than ten residential blocks and the

Lincoln car as well. Local citizens were invited to take souvenirs but few pieces of the car remain.

Designed for elegance yet never used by its owner in life; railroad executives' private car, then used by track workers; made of the finest materials, yet burned in a grass fire, President Lincoln's private car "United States" holds an enigmatic and fascinating place in railroad history.

In nearly dilapidated condition the coach rested after its return from Colorado in the Union Pacific's Omaha yards until 1903.
(Union Pacific Museum Collection)

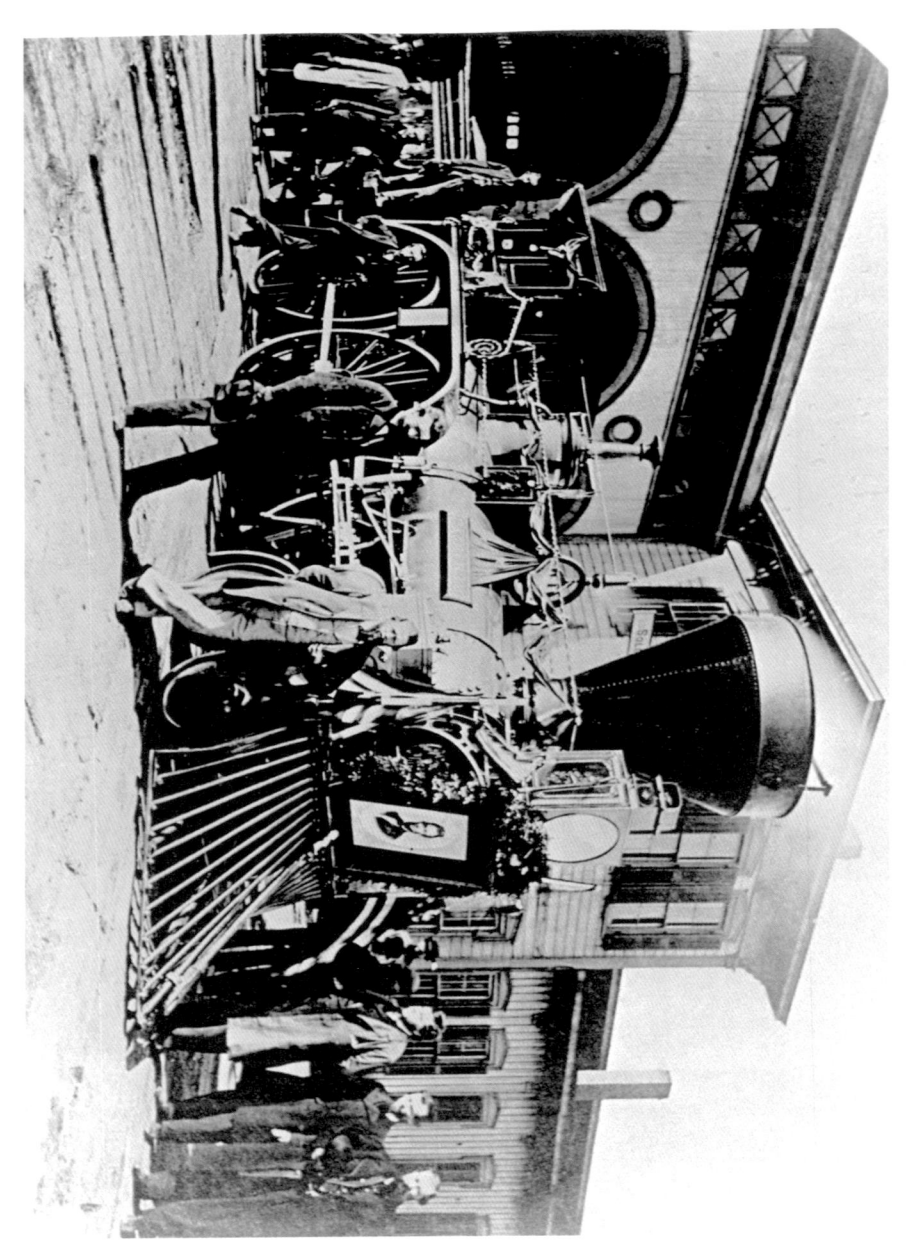

Probably more than twenty different locomotives were used on the trip. Built by the Cuyahoga Steam Furnace Works (Cleveland) the "Nashville" was the most decorated engine on the trip. (Library of Congress)

16

A variety of locomotives pulled the funeral special. Since locomotive design was still in its infancy there were few motive power standards and most engines stayed close to their home shops. Probably more than twenty engines were used on the trip. One of the more spectacular locomotives was the Cleveland, Columbus and Cincinnati RR's Nashville. Built by Cuyahoga Steam Furnace Works in 1852 the engine featured Rogers variable cutoff valve gear driven by six eccentric cranks on the front driver axle. Well-liked by engineers, the Nashville had canted cylinders and a whistle mounted atop the hollow bell bracket. Draped in bunting, tassels and wreaths, it featured three portraits of Lincoln and two specially designed flags with a large central star for the President and smaller stars for the states in the Union.

By military order, the train consisted of nine cars with the presidential car the second from the last. At many stops state governors, dignitaries, and military officers would join the honored few as others left. One exception to the timetable was the stop in Michigan City, IN where the train waited for Illinois dignitaries to journey by buggy from Chicago to join the train for its honored trip back into Chicago. The ladies of Michigan City had prepared a sumptuous whitefish breakfast and while the politicians ate, the long-delayed train promptly left. The startled officials had to commandeer another engine to catch up with the train.

For their services each of the twenty-seven official train guards from the Veterans (Invalid) Reserve Corps was awarded the Medal of Honor only to have it rescinded and made illegal to wear when Congress, in 1917, limited the medal for only extreme valor in combat.

For twenty days from Lincoln's assassination to his burial the entire nation was transfixed by possibly the largest traditional funeral in American History.

(ABOVE) Extending almost fifteen feet, the finished model exhibit represents the funeral as it might have appeared in Springfield, IL. It was nearly four and one half years in construction and represents thousands of hours of modeling time. (Ed Bunting)

(RIGHT) The honor guards were handcrafted by Ron Lofman of Madison, WI. From the names of the actual guards they appeared to be of Irish and German descent so Ron created figures with appropriate ethnic facial features. Each is dressed in the Uniform of the Veteran Reserve Corps who were special volunteers for light duty, band and honor guards. The bandsman in the rear has the facial features of the late Gordon Odegard, president of the lst Brigade Band of Broadhead, WI, a Civil War re-enactors group. (W. Wesolowski)

19

The large size model of the President's car "United States" is almost four feet long. (Ed Bunting)

The Lincoln Train is coming...The 1995 Model

The "founding father" of the Lincoln train was the late Thomas Dyba who studied and wrote about the Lincoln Home in Springfield, IL. Tom built a one-twelfth scale model of the only home Lincoln ever owned which is located at the Lincoln Library and Museum, Springfield, Illinois. The scale house is most impressive but also too heavy and large to move comfortably. It was his thought that this large scale model of Abraham Lincoln's private coach and a traveling exhibit of the funeral train would compliment the already extensive (80,000 pieces) IBC Lincoln collection. Knowing that IBC chemistry professor, Wayne Wesolowski, is a railroad enthusiast and model builder he shared his vision with him. Wesolowski eventually committed to the idea and a campus committee was assembled and the project planned. Part of the goal for the project is to evoke a sense of patriotism while commemorating the 130th anniversary of the death of one of our nation's most-admired presidents.

After two years of research, including contacting virtually every museum and historical society along the original route, John Haines of Haines Miniature Machine, Benicia, CA was commissioned by Kalmbach publishing, Waukesha, WI to prepare the scale engineering drawings for the presidential car, the locomotive and the tender. John's close attention to detail and knowledge of machinery allowed the finished models to be the most perfect recreations possible based on photos and historical documents available. Once the project was announced on Lincoln's birthday 1993, Lincoln scholars, Lincoln aficionados, Civil War enthusiasts, collectors, historians, curators, citizens across the country, volunteered information, artifacts, family photos, family histories and memories, old books, possible leads and suggestions. As a result of very generous people, not all listed in the limited space of the acknowledgement page, all the parts began to fit together. Even seemingly seriously conflicting historic newspaper reports were resolved with some detective work and "a little help from our friends."

The Presidential Car "United States"

The presidential car, "United States," was the first model to be constructed and when it came to painting the documented color was "rich chocolate brown" and "claret red." Without color photographs from 1865 how could these two reports be resolved? At the suggestion of IBC nutritionist, C. Matis, the history of chocolate was researched and the discovery made that "chocolate" in 1865 was strictly a drink. Cocoa beans used to produce it were treated with lye, a process termed "Dutching" giving a reddish maroon color to the drink. So chocolate and claret were compatible terms after all. The California and Nevada State Railroad Museums were both helpful in identifying the closest "railroad" color to maroon for our car. The scale tassels are copies of one of the original spun metal tassels from the presidential car, the stars holding the bunting in place are patterned after a real silver medallion in a private collection. The frosted windows are miniature photo reproductions of an actual window from the original car.

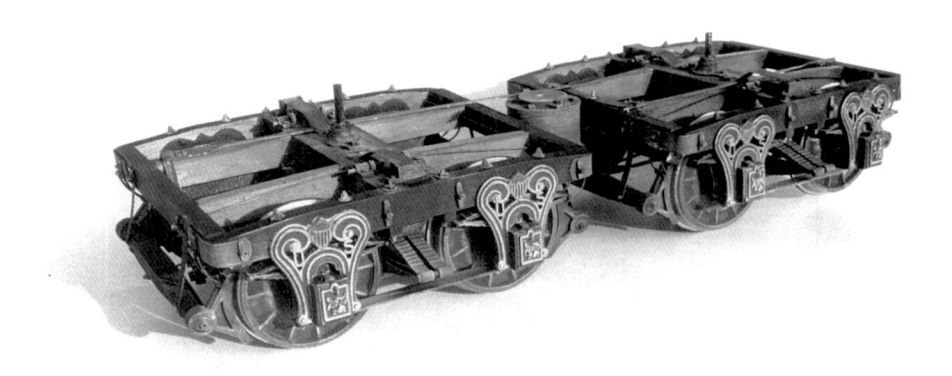

The miniature trucks or undercarriage contain 725 parts including all the brake rigging and springs. India rubber pads were used in many places for a more comfortable ride. The wheels have extra wide tread to traverse the various rail spacings that were not standardized across America.

In model construction it is always a pleasant surprise when an "easy" substitution for a model component is discovered. In the case of the roof vents on the presidential car the inner plastic liners (pull tabs) of some canola oil bottles cleaned and sprayed black were just such a find. The little doormat (undoubtedly added to prevent an excess of dirt and mud from the rainy April weather) was simulated with a kitchen pot scrubber.

In many cases, the model is constructed in the same fashion as the prototype. Unfortunately there was no easy kitchen substitute for the yards of black bunting. Black fabric was cut, soaked in a mixture of glue and water, draped to size, pinned in place, allowed to dry and attached to the car with the tiny silver star medallions, photoetched from an original. The roof, too, followed prototype construction using canvas-like fabric, soaked in paint and sprinkled with sifted sand to provide fireproofing against errant embers from the smokestack of the woodburning locomotive and to give some traction for walking.

Because the fringe along the roofline needed to be consistent in length original attempts to sew individual pieces of thread were abandoned and a much simpler precise method of "row raveling" of a silky loosely woven fabric employed and then finished with silver spray. Raveling was again used to create the fringe at the bottom of each black ribbon panel and then painted silver with a fine brush.

In recreating the ornate railings repeated patterns were a great help. Rolled round solder was the basic material used to make a "master" pattern. A rubber mold was created and then polyurethane copies produced, assembled to form the proper arrangement of the "metalwork," painted and attached. Polyurethane is the liquid plastic material used consistently in all the models because of its durability and ease in machining, filing and sanding.

Because the model is dollhouse scale (1in = 1ft) a ready-made doorknob and keyhole were used for the car doors.

The model roof vents are the inner liners from a canola oil bottle. The small frosted glass windows are photographic reductions of an actual piece of glass from the real car. The scoop-shaped devices are made from little plastic funnels and were used to move air about the car. The roof is cloth soaked in paint and sprinkled with sand for fireproofing and traction for walking. (W. Wesolowski)

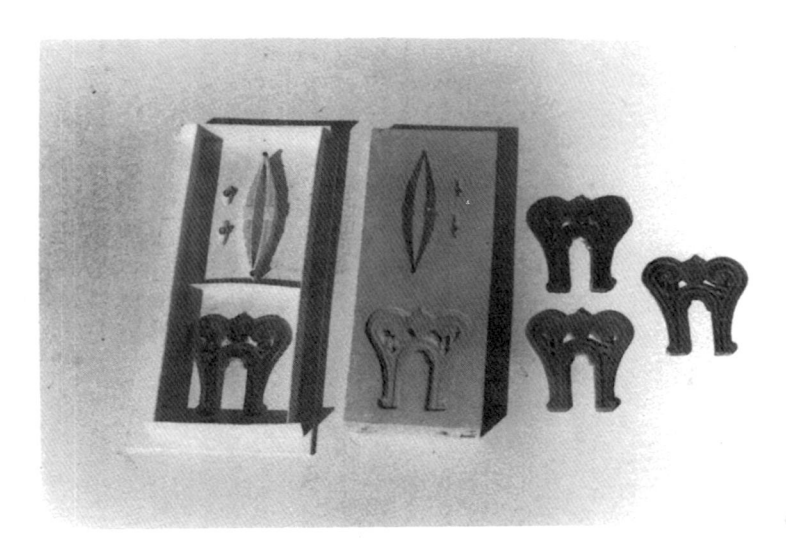

The casting process: (left) Master pattern in mold box. (center) Mold made from liquid rubber poured into mold box. (right) Multiple copies made from liquid plastic poured into mold. (W. Wesolowski)

24

Toward the rear of the "United States" one can see the end windows drawn from photos of the car and the tiny railings cast in plastic from rolled solder masters. The tiny stars holding the bunting in place are photoetched copies from real pieces.

On the side of the car, the presidential seal can be viewed, painted by BU Art Professor William Scarlato. (W. Wesolowski)

Model maker Professor Wayne Wesolowski stands proudly with his finished model of the "Nashville." (S. Wesolowski)

The Locomotive "Nashville"

The Locomotive, "Nashville," was chosen from among perhaps twenty diminutive engines that were used between Washington, DC and Springfield, IL because it was rather unusual and there were THREE historic photographs available of it. That is three times as many as most of the others. Modern steam locomotives are traditionally deep black but Civil War engine designers used a full palette of colors. Red wheels, blue bodies and bold brass and iron straps were not uncommon with even a dash of pink or purple. After much consideration a conservative green and cream basic color combination was chosen. Again, without color photographs, this was a difficult decision.

The locomotive, surprisingly, has no brakes, only a set of hand-cranked wooden pads on the rear trucks of the tender. The boiler base was constructed using a piece of plastic water pipe wrapped in thin metal foil held in place with brass strips. The headlight reflector is a small flashlight. The decorative artwork on the headlight box is a combination of carnations and buckeye leaves. Drawn oversize from photographs, colored according to the Ohio state flower and tree (as the Cleveland engine manufacturer did in 1852), color photocopied, the artwork was reduced to size.

The "cowcatcher" or, more correctly, the pilot, is a collection of small copper tubes, cut and soldered into place. This little engine was an engineering marvel of its time with an elaborate set of levers, arms and valves to accurately meter steam into the engine's cylinders. All the complex engineering features are included in the model. The frame was made piece by piece from hardwood. The valve gear all function as the prototype but the model simply rolls and is not actually powered. The tender contains a supply of hedge clipping "firewood." Over three thousand rivets add detail to its styrene wrapper. Plastic castings are used for the driving wheels and tender trucks.

The screen covering on the smokestack was yet another challenge because of the pattern of the screening.

Although hidden inside the body the complete valve gear was created for the model. All of these arms and levers move so that the steam could be accurately metered into the cylinders. For the model, these parts were made from styrene plastic or brass.

Very unusual trucks for the tender have the body actually riding directly on the outside springs. The tender tank of water is a block of wood wrapped with a thin plastic sheet which was punched with thousands of tiny rivets. (W. Wesolowski)

28

Rather than having the common rectangular openings it had a diamond pattern. Quite by accident a raid on the kitchen (a seemingly consistent source of odd modeling items) produced a cook's spatter screen with the right size pattern. It was flat and the smokestack screen is domed. How to form the dome without creasing the screen? Son Steve, a basketball player, with one slamdunk accomplished the mission—a nicely rounded indentation without any kinks.

The special flags were silkscreened onto linen handkerchiefs by a local T-shirt shop and mounted on wooden food skewers. The draping and mourning badges were simulated using finely pleated black and white fabric and stitched into place. The wreath of flowers around the portrait of Lincoln was fashioned from scale greenery and miniature flowers, again patterned on a magnifying glass view of one of the few photographs available.

The portraits of Lincoln (reduced by copy machine process) used on the locomotive were identified as the proper image by Lloyd Ostendorf, noted Lincoln image scholar.

Using a three-inch plastic water pipe for the boiler the Nashville begins to come together. (W. Wesolowski)

The miniature hearse driver holds his plastic steeds steady as the honor guard brings Mr. Lincoln's coffin to the coach. (W. Wesolowski)

The Hearse and Horses

The hearse model is a scale reproduction of the ornate vehicle loaned by the mayor of St. Louis, MO to the city of Springfield, IL and based on a single photograph. This time there were no questions of color. Everything is funeral black and silver. Because of its size and almost exclusively plastic construction it is by far the lightest and easiest to move component of the exhibit. The repeat patterns are easily identified—the window sections, the arched filigree, pillars and even the upside down torches on the side of the coach. The plumes are simulated with miniature Christmas trees turned upside down, cut to shape, sprayed black and mounted in an ornate holder composed of mostly jewelry beads and findings. The bunting is a different style than that used on the presidential car so a combination of stiffened fabric and ribbon was used. The tassels are handmade from silver embroidery thread. Simulating the leather on the driver's seat is the reverse side of black patching fabric from a sewing supply shop.

The gathered cloth panel on the side of the coach posed a vexing problem. Real cloth proved too heavy a material to properly gather. Instead, a large clay sheet was formed and then with a linoleum gouge the radiating ribs were cut into clay. A mold of this pattern was made and plastic castings created for the finished model. Even though only two were cast this was the only way they could be made.

The horses, purchased from a toy shop, underwent model surgery. Their necks, knees and ankles were softened and moved into more realistic positions. Their bodies were then painted black and eyes glossed. Blankets were cut and fitted from a black wool scarf and again controlled fraying or raveling was used to create the fringe which was silvered by hand.

A local stable explained just how the reins were arranged in pairs and threaded back to the hands of the horse driver who needed to have full control, especially for a stately funeral. Thin soft metal reins droop authentically like leather.

32

The Coffin and the Figures

Lincoln's coffin was custom-made from fine wood then covered in black broadcloth and decorated with silver tacks, stars and large handles. Patterned after a photo of a replica owned by the Illinois Funeral Directors' Association the model casket features more than 800 silver tacks and has the texture of cloth even though the model is not actually covered with it. One of the inconsistencies readily noticeable in dollhouse displays is the fabric used for curtains and upholstery. The pattern must be to scale but, just as importantly, it must also have a scale texture. Using actual broadcloth to cover a base for replicating the coffin would seem logical but the texture produced would be too coarse. The fine texture on the coffin was created by gently scratching the surface with an 80-grit sandpaper in a crisscross pattern like cloth.

Ron Lofman of Madison, WI is the creator of the scale figures used in the exhibit. Researching uniforms at the Grand Army of the Republic Museum in Wisconsin, he was able to accurately detail the shoe laces, hat embroidery, uniform color, and armbands. Studying the surnames of the twenty-seven members of the Veterans (Invalid) Reserve Corps, Ron determined that most of the names indicated Irish and German heritage. Features of these two ethnic groups were added to the model soldiers. The civilian on the back of the presidential car is Ward Hill Lamon, the only person to accompany President Lincoln on both his complete inaugural and funeral trips. Two other figures are also personalized. The bandsman is patterned after the late Gordon Odegard who served as president and drum major of the 1st Brigade Band of Broadhead, WI. This group uses authentic Civil War instruments and arrangements. The other "personality" is model maker and author, Wayne Wesolowski, as the engineer.

About The Model Makers

Wayne Wesolowski has been building transportation-related models as a hobby for more than 40 years. Beginning with Lionel trains, he worked with his father on many model layouts. A professor of chemistry at Illinois Benedictine College (IBC), Lisle, Illinois, and now teaching at The University of Arizona. His spare time is spent crafting miniature recreations of railroad and old industrial scenes. Teaching many pre-medical courses, he finds working with his hands a pleasant diversion.

Each project is a special adventure in bringing back to life part of American industrial history that depicts scenes of people and activities. Wayne's modeling work is on display at the National Railroad Museum. RailAmerica, the West Chicago Historical Museum, the Batavia (IL) Depot Museum, and the Chicago Museum of Science and Industry among others. His unique skills as a chemist and modeler are combined in many of the special techniques used in his projects. For example, for the Lincoln Train project tiny parts were photoengraved during a summer school chemistry class using the sun for exposures. The technique of acid etching was also safely completed in the chemistry lab. Many of the 725 detail parts for the wheels and undercarriage are cast using liquid plastics in flexible rubber molds then painted and aged to look like old iron. As Wayne points out, the Lincoln Train Project could not have been completed without using the principals of chemistry—" Better things in miniature, through chemistry."

A more than 55-year member of the National Model Railroad Association, Wayne frequently lectures on model building and the Lincoln Train to clubs and groups of all types. He likes to educate through his models and truly believes that building historically accurate models is recreating a little bit of reality.

Steve Wesolowski received his first payment for model building from Model Railroader when he was in second grade for a scratch-built fence article. Having completed college graduation and graduate school in theoretical chemistry he has more than thirteen years experience building scale models. Because Wayne does most of his model building during the summer it was convenient to have Steve help during vacation time. For the Lincoln Train project Steve became almost a full-time partner because of his vast experience and "secret" casting techniques.

The little spare time that Steve has is used out on the golf course or in the gym playing basketball.

Wayne Wesolowski, PhD has been building transportation and industrial history models for more than forty years. His work has been exhibited at the Chicago Museum of Science and Industry, RailAmerica, the California State Railroad Museum and the National Railroad Museum among many others. One of his favorites is his traveling exhibit of the Abraham Lincoln Funeral Train sponsored by the Chicago Tribune McCormick Foundation. He especially enjoys building models of miniature machine tools and pipe organs.

Along with his wife, Mary Cay, he has written nearly 175 articles and four books on model building. He stars in two video tapes on model making produced by Kalmbach Publishing and shown nationally on PBS. Good Morning America selected and showed part of one tape as an example of video education. Bob Hundman of Mainline Modeler Magazine said of Wayne, "He's always leading those of us who like scratchbuilding down new roads. He's a very inventive modeler."

"It is my opinion that no historical model or reproduction of the *Nashville* or the *United States* would be accurate or complete without the services of Dr. Wesolowski." —Bill Leto, Lionel Trains LTD

Always looking for ways to educate through models Wayne has created teaching exhibits for museums and clients across the country. He has a research PhD in Chemistry and continues to teach undergraduates at The University of Arizona.

For more information please contact
Wayne Wesolowski
Box 896
Cortaro, AZ 85652